Fortune 500 Exe
Praise Bill Butterworth

"Bill Butterworth makes me laugh, but more importantly he makes me think. Bill is much more than an inspirational speaker.... He is a locomotive of energy.... No wonder I like him so much."

—JACK KEMP, former vice presidential candidate and founder and chairman of Kemp Partners

"We are impressed with Bill's style, content, and ability to connect with the audience. He's an outstanding communicator—versatile in approach and content."

—WALT DISNEY COMPANY

"Our entire management team enjoys how appropriate the subject of work-life balance is for the organization."

—FORD MOTOR COMPANY

"In a hard-charging business environment it's difficult to maintain perspective; Bill Butterworth's ideas on balance are very appropriate."

—AMERICAN EXPRESS

"A home run! The mix of humor and message was just what we hoped for."

—BANK OF AMERICA

"Wonderful! Wow!"

—MassMutual Insurance

"Bill Butterworth is terrific on the subject of work-life balance. He brings joy and laughter to senior executives; I would recommend him to any group seeking to improve morale or simply to develop key members' leadership skills."

—DaimlerChrysler

"Bill is dynamite! He has the rare ability to relax his audience with humor, followed by a powerful, riveting message driven home forcefully."

—Young Presidents' Organization

"An outstanding message. Bill Butterworth is helping our employees lead balanced lives."

—PNC Bank

"Bill Butterworth's contributions helped kick us into high gear! He was the highest-rated speaker of our entire conference...a smashing success!"

—BlueCross BlueShield

"Fantastic! Bill Butterworth put smiles on our faces, touched our hearts, and reminded us of what is really important in life."

—American Institute of Certified Public Accountants

"Bill Butterworth's insight into management and corporate relations regarding employer-employee teamwork and business-to-client relationships assisted my firm to grow 25 percent in one year versus the projected 12 percent. I highly recommend Bill's strategies to every CEO. His insight into how people relate to each other is second to none!"

—HAR-BRO Incorporated

"Bill's time with our company was the best motivational experience we've had. He articulated our vision and balanced it with values we respect."

—Morton Industrial Group

"Perfect mix of humor and message. How can we possibly thank Bill Butterworth enough!"

—California Credit Union League

"Bill's blend of humor, insight, and storytelling left us with unforgettable mental pictures of how to manage change."

—Tranzact Systems

"Bill Butterworth keeps us on the edge of our seats. The issue of balance between our obligations to family, work, and personal time is important; rarely has that message been offered with such energy or received with such enthusiasm. Bill's message is timely and presented in such a way that resonates."

—Council of Alumni Association Executives

"Bill Butterworth's participation and contribution are definitely a key factor to success. His enthusiasm, sense of humor, and ability to involve the audience—all wonderful!"

—Knott's Berry Farm

"Bill has given us many points to consider. Time with him seems like time shared with a longtime friend. He brings humor and personality."

—Deutsche Financial Services

"A 10 in every way. Bill is interesting, amusing, and insightful, and his ideas go a long way in helping our membership."

—Meeting Professionals International

"Great style. Bill Butterworth had us in the palm of his hand and left us feeling happy, satisfied, and with a new outlook on life!"

—AIMS Logistics

"Outstanding! Bill is super!"

—Gulf Power

"Bill's evaluations were overwhelmingly positive, and many cited his presentation as the conference highlight!"

—National Association of Catering Executives

"Outstanding presentation...terrific."

—Electrical Apparatus Service Association

Building Successful Teams

Building Successful Teams

Bill Butterworth

New York London Toronto Sydney Auckland

A CURRENCY BOOK
PUBLISHED BY DOUBLEDAY

On-the-Fly Guide to Building Successful Teams will be published simultaneously by WaterBrook Press.

Published in the United States by Doubleday, an imprint of The Doubleday Broadway Publishing Group, a division of Random House, Inc., New York.

www.currencybooks.com

Details in some anecdotes and stories have been changed to protect the identities of the persons involved.

Published in association with the literary agency of Alive Communications, Inc.,
7680 Goddard Street, Suite 200, Colorado Springs, Colorado 80920,
www.alivecommunications.com

Library of Congress Cataloging-in-Publication Data
Butterworth, Bill.
On-the-fly guide to...building successful teams : maximize performance from those around you / Bill Butterworth.—1st ed.
p. cm.
Includes bibliographical references.
1. Teams in the workplace. I. Title: Building successful teams. II. Title.
HD66.B88 2006
658.4'022—dc22 2006001041

ISBN-13: 978-0-385-51969-4
ISBN-10: 0-385-51969-9

PRINTED IN THE UNITED STATES OF AMERICA

10 9 8 7 6 5 4 3 2

First Edition

For Kathi

Love with wings

Contents

Acknowledgments

A book is always a collaborative effort. Therefore, I have many people to thank who have invested in my life. In countless ways they have made a great contribution to this book.

Don Pape sparked my creative fire with the original idea for a series entitled "On-the-Fly." As my literary agent and friend, he has always been willing to listen to my ramblings. He deserves an extra pat on the back for being so patient with me. All the folks at Alive Communications are fantastic, and I owe a special debt of gratitude to *Lee Hough.*

The people at Doubleday have been wonderfully kind to me. I am so indebted to *Michael Palgon, Roger Scholl,* and *Sarah Rainone* for their loving care in handling this project.

The gang at WaterBrook Press is amazing. I have spent a fair amount of time with them, and they are still publishing me! To name a few: *Steve Cobb, Dudley Delffs, Mick Silva, Jessica Barnes, Carol Bartley, Brian McGinley, Ginia Hairston, Jan Walker, Kevin Hallwyler, Lori Addicott, Joel Kneedler, Leah McMahan,* and *Alice Crider* are all part of one fantastic team.

I have wonderful friends in my life. I am so grateful to people like *Lee* and *Leslie Strobel, Joe* and *Molly Davis, Mike* and *Marcia Scott, Ron* and *Kay Nelson, Bob* and *Barb Ludwig, Gary* and *Linda Bender, Jim* and *Ines Franklin, Al* and *Anita Manley, Val* and *Linda Giannini, Todd* and *Cheryl Jensen, Ruben* and *Trish*

Guzman, and *Ken* and *Judy Gire* for their valuable contributions on a regular basis.

Many business leaders have believed in me from the start, and I must acknowledge their constant insight and encouragement. I know I will miss some, but special thanks to *Bill Morton, Mike Sime, Mike Regan, Mark Zoradi, Bill Coyne, Brad Quayle, Dave Nelson, Dee Tolles, Dave Stone, Dan Lungren, Joe Ahern, Bob Buford, John Pearson, Tim Cass, Ralph Jones, Rich Caturano, Jim Gwinn, Keith Harrell, Mark Thomas, Rick Warren, Bob Harron, Bill Hybels, Jon Singley, Ron Whitmill, Joe Belew,* and *Mark Laudeman.*

I also want to thank all the speakers' bureaus that have faithfully represented me over the years. I am greatly indebted to you, not just for the business, but also for your friendship.

My children (and now grandchildren) have hung in with me through good times and bad. You are my great treasure. Thank you for all you have taught me.

And finally, my dear wife, *Kathi.* You know all about me and choose to live with me anyway. Thanks so very much. You're amazing.

Introduction

Everything I Know About Teamwork I Learned at Carnegie Hall

"Dad, we're gonna sing at Carnegie Hall!"

So bellowed my sixteen-year-old son, John, as he ran down the hall of our California home. An eleventh grader, John was a member of his high-school choir. They had previously submitted an audition tape to join a five-hundred-voice all-American high-school honors choir, and John had just learned that they had been accepted.

Most folks I know have heard of Carnegie Hall. Few have ever been there.

When I walked through the doors on that cold winter night in March, I made two discoveries. One, Carnegie Hall is not as big as I had imagined. Don't get me wrong, it's big—a couple thousand seats at least. But to a guy who has attended too many concerts in arenas and stadiums, it seemed almost small.

Two, the Carnegie Hall stage doesn't have a curtain. All onstage activity comes and goes through a set of double doors on the right side of the stage. I'm guessing it has something to do with the hall's acoustic perfection, but there is no big, heavy, velvet curtain like you'd expect. This is not a problem aesthetically, except that, between acts, what would be considered backstage movement is in full view.

The high-school choir was the main attraction, but obviously it needed an opening act. And who better to open for the five-hundred-voice all-American high-school honors choir than the five-hundred-voice all-American *elementary*-school honors choir?

That's right, five hundred eight-, nine-, and ten-year-olds marched onto the stage and proceeded to sing their set. I saw proud parents beaming from every seat in the hall. Many people wept as the children sang (I'll let you determine why their singing would reduce an adult to tears), and I quickly decided that this concert could not fail.

Everyone in the hall was related to one of the performers.

The elementary-school choir performed its last piece, received well-deserved applause, and marched off the stage.

Now for the good part, I thought and smiled. *The high schoolers.*

Not yet. After the first choir was completely offstage, two very tiny children strolled onstage with the smallest violins I had ever seen. Their instruments looked like knickknacks you might display on your coffee table back home. Nonetheless, these two talented mini-people played a beautiful classical piece to the delight of several thousand ears. The applause was deafening as they wandered offstage, their little violins in tow.

The time had finally arrived. The double doors opened wide, and out of them came five hundred beautiful teenagers. The young ladies wore formal gowns, the young men tuxedos. I craned my neck like a giraffe and looked for John. But as student after student glided onstage, I could not find my son. The first row was in place, but no John. The second row, no John. As the third row assembled, I realized what was happening. The choir was lining up front row to back row, shortest to tallest.

John is six feet four inches tall.

"Oh no," I groaned. Most certainly, John would be sentenced to the back row.

Sure enough, after approximately 483 people walked on stage, John appeared at the double doors. My chest swelled with pride, but I was still disappointed that he was in the back row. *This isn't at all how I imagined it,* I thought. *It was gonna be John up front. John with his 499 backup singers. Johnny and the Pips, live at Carnegie Hall.*

It was at that moment my disappointment turned into joy. As John took his place on the back row, he happened to be dead center. A spotlight shone on him alone, lighting him up like a Roman candle. No one else looked like he looked, at least to me. He had an angelic glow, a halo, like in one of those Renaissance paintings of Jesus.

The choir was now in place. The double doors were closed in anticipation of the conductor's appearance. The excitement was palpable. All eyes were on the double doors. But they did not open. "Where's the conductor?" parents whispered to one another. "What are we waiting for?"

The wait seemed interminable. Even the choir was getting restless. After what seemed like an hour, the double doors opened to show us a middle-aged man in his best blue suit. As he walked onstage, we could not keep our enthusiasm to ourselves.

We applauded.

We applauded like there was no tomorrow.

We applauded so wildly we had to stand to accurately show our appreciation for this unforgettable moment.

So amid this thunderous standing ovation, imagine our surprise when we discovered that the man strolling toward center stage was not the conductor.

He was a stagehand.

The two little violinists had neglected to take their music stand with them when they finished their number, so we were wildly applauding the Carnegie Hall stagehand! He picked up the stand, walked back offstage, and the double doors closed once again.

Almost immediately, however, the double doors reopened, and a handsome man in white tie and tails proudly marched to the center of the stage. This time it was the conductor, but he was greeted with lukewarm applause. We had given it all up for the stagehand, so we didn't have much left.

I was immediately struck with the thought, *When was the last time I was at a concert where we gave the stagehand a standing ovation?* Clearly he was important to the evening's festivities. The concert could not proceed without his clearing the stage. He was every bit as vital in his way as the conductor. But in our world, we tend to applaud only the conductor, only the quarterback, only the CEO, forgetting all the other people responsible for a team's success. Examples from business abound. Even the design of an organizational chart, though necessary for efficient business practices, states, or at least implies, that there is a pecking order in the company. Those higher up the ladder are more important than those on the lower rungs.

As the concert unfolded, I knew I was observing something special. Beyond the obvious pride of seeing my son's performance, I knew I was also witnessing teamwork in action. Every person on that stage was making a contribution; each one was necessary for the complete success of the team.

This book explores the many ways you can maximize your own team's effectiveness. We'll talk about team leaders and team members, new teams and old teams, big teams and small teams. We'll talk about your relationships within your business team and the responsibilities your team places on you. My contention is that whether you're a CEO or a personal assistant, the sooner you realize you are a critical member of a dynamic working team, the more efficient you will be.

I will explain how you can determine the *needs* of your teammates, overcome the *barriers* to teamwork, and recognize the *great traits* of effective teams. Throughout the book, you will find helpful Team Tips to reflect upon, as well as questions and exercises that will help you put the book's lessons into practice.

I wrote this to be read during a short plane ride, to jump-start your thinking. Be warned: although it's a quick read, it just might change for good the way you view teamwork and your position as a team member. Yet I believe that if you practice these truths, you will learn how to increase your effectiveness as well as the effectiveness of all those around you.

And then there's no telling what you'll be able to accomplish.

One

The Three Great Needs of Team Members

Before you can focus your attention on increasing the effectiveness of your team, you need to examine what each member brings to the mix. Besides a laundry list of strengths, gifts, and skills, every human being on your team brings with him or her a set of *needs.* The beauty of successful teamwork is that it not only accomplishes the overall goals and objectives of the team, but it also helps meet the individual needs of each teammate.

So what are some of the needs a team member might bring to the table?

Psychologists from many different schools of thought seem to agree when it comes to the basic needs of individuals. Some add a few more items to the list, but most include the three I'll discuss in this chapter: a sense of *belonging,* a sense of *worth,* and a sense of *competence.*

THE NEED TO BELONG

For some of us, our earliest recollections of teamwork are from neighborhood games. Whether our groups gathered at a field, in a back alley, or in a sandlot, the ritual of choosing sides to play a game is an almost universal experience.

Since I was an overly large child growing up, I have mostly painful memories of this experience. Stated simply, because I was fat, I was almost always the last kid chosen to play ball. The exception was during football season, when the coaches or other players saw the value in having some extra tonnage on the offensive line. I can even remember being chosen first a time or two. My strategy was simple: hike the ball and roll over. I never failed to stop the defense in their tracks, leaving my team open to score at will!

But the rest of the year was dominated by basketball and baseball. The only way a big boy is desirable in baseball is if he can knock the cover off the ball. Regrettably, my extra weight slowed down my swing so significantly that I rarely got a chance to make direct contact with the ball. (Actually I had a good hit once. I started swinging at the first pitch and solidly connected with the second.)

We all know that kids can be cruel to one another, and this was certainly true during my childhood. When choosing sides, not only was I usually last, but I was forced to endure a horrible scene that went something like this:

"Okay, there are only two guys left, so I'll pick Mark," one of the captains would say. "That means you have Billy."

"I didn't pick him," the other captain would retort.

"I know. But he's the last one, so you have to take him."

"I don't want him."

"You have to take him."

"Who says I have to take him?"

"You have to take him 'cause it's your pick, and he's the last kid."

"But I don't want him."

This would go on for several minutes until the protesting captain would grudgingly take me, muttering something under his breath about how the only thing I was good for was playing backstop.

Can you feel my pain? I just wanted to be part of the team—any team.

A wonderful group of individuals make up your team, and they all have something in common: an innate yearning to belong. Some are more in touch with this feeling than others, but we all possess it.

This longing can explain why, as adults, when we look back on our youth and point out our most treasured memories, many of us gravitate toward experiences we shared with others. Just the other day a friend of mine was looking back fondly on his high-school days. An exceptional athlete, he recalled winning an individual cross-country event, as well as the year his football team won the division championship. Which was the greater memory for my friend? "No question about it—the football championship," he told me. Why? "Because it was a team effort."

The football team, the marching band, the science club—all are group activities that are built around the concept of *belonging.*

I recently made a presentation on teamwork to a group of middle managers in Miami, Florida. After the session, a woman in her early forties approached the platform to speak with me. We shook hands, exchanged pleasantries, and then she got right to it. "Your speech caused a light bulb to go off in my brain this morning," she chuckled.

"What did I say that caused that response?" I inquired.

"For the first time in all the years I've been working with this company, I realized why I *love* working here."

"Why?"

"Because it feels like family," she said with a warm smile on her face. "I have a wonderful husband and kids at home—don't get me wrong. But I love the people I work with. My job is more than a place to pick up a paycheck. We look out for each other, and it creates an atmosphere that feels like family. We all belong."

THE NEED TO FEEL WORTHY

I have a friend who travels around the country speaking on issues of self-worth. I love one of his maxims, not only because it rings true, but also because it's practically poetic.

"How would I describe life at its best?" he asks his audience. "I would answer that question in this manner: *nothing to lose, nothing to prove, nothing to hide.*"

Isn't that great? That's what a sense of worth provides. I can go for it; I have nothing to lose. Risk taking is a sign of a person with a strong sense of positive self-worth. Taking risks says, "I am secure enough in who I am that I can make bold moves without losing my self-confidence." It says, "If I fail, I will just pick myself up and try it again a different way!"

A risktaker thinks like this. He's secure enough in who he is, so there's no need to prove himself to anyone. She doesn't base her self-worth on how others view her. He doesn't need approval to feel worth within himself. It doesn't hurt if you like her, but it is not the basis of her self-image.

A person with nothing to prove is the quintessential team player.

Imagine your life were an open book—with no secrets buried away on some dusty shelf. Most of us can only imagine how freeing this type of life must be. A life without secrets? That sounds too good to be true! But it is possible. It is attainable. It requires gut-wrenching honesty, but the payoff is huge. A team made up of vulnerable, transparent individuals is a uniquely effective team indeed.

If you create an environment of open, honest communication, your team will grow together. And a team that is growing together is a team that feels good about themselves. Effective teams stimulate healthy self-worth.

Mitchell knows the value of this concept. He told me recently, "I was very guarded at my workplace. I didn't want anyone knowing what was going on in my world. I operated on a 'need to know basis' with just about everyone in the company. Fortunately, that all changed."

"What prompted the change?" I asked.

"Actually, it was my performance review by my superior," he replied. "I scored high on most of the scales, but he rated me low on open communication. As we talked, I began to see that, naturally, some areas of my personal life are off limits, but overall I could be much more open in my communication style. I started sharing a bit more with my co-workers and made the most wonderful discovery—they really care about me! It feels so good not having secrets and restrictions that hold me back from being all I can be."

THE NEED TO FEEL COMPETENT

The third great need of our lives is the need to feel competent. We want to feel as though we are making a contribution to the group with which we're connected. Whether it is a family, an athletic team, a management team, or a business organization, we want to do our part to help it succeed.

Before I go any further, I want to be sure we get one thing nailed down. Every person who reads these words has tremendous worth. Every one of you can experience the wonderful sense of belonging that comes from being connected with a team. And every one of you can make a positive contribution to that team. Your effort should come from your skill set or your strengths, whichever words you use to describe that treasure chest of talents that make you unique. And it is that uniqueness that makes you so desirable to your team.

But unless you have confidence in your uniqueness, it's highly unlikely your team will. I'm not suggesting unchecked pride and arrogance, but you shouldn't get in the habit of making self-deprecating remarks, either. Instead, I'm suggesting you make an objective, honest, realistic assessment of who you are, including strengths and areas that need improvement.

If you have never looked at what makes you unique, you need to make a commitment to yourself to do so in the immediate future. There are many wonderful tools that provide inventories to assess your skill set, and I encourage you to explore them. A visit to your Human Resources department or your nearest bookstore will most likely yield a bounty of measuring devices.

But if you don't want to get HR involved, just take a blank sheet of paper and begin writing down the tasks you like doing on the left side and the tasks you dislike on the right. If you could have any job in the world, what would the ideal job look like? You will soon discover there are reasons why you gravitate to certain assignments and avoid others—they directly relate to your skill set. This is also a great place to insert feedback from those who are closest to you—family, friends, and immediate co-workers. They can spot qualities in you that you might fail to see.

Effective teams are made up of a variety of skill sets. There is a leader, of course. But you also want someone who shares the vision, someone who will work the plan, someone who can communicate well, someone who is highly organized, someone who can think outside the box, and a whole host of other roles. Each role specifically relates to that team member's core competence, which in turn leads to maximum efficiency and, ultimately, superior team performance.

And that's the sort of excellence great teams are made of.

PART ONE

The Four Great Barriers to Teamwork

Two

The Barrier of Personal Insecurity

Just as team members' personal needs must be met to maximize team performance, experts agree there are also four shared barriers that must be overcome to release any team's full potential. If your team can overcome this quartet of roadblocks, you will make great strides toward effective teamwork.

The first barrier is personal insecurity. This barrier limits your team's effectiveness as a result of each member's personal issues. It's a common struggle; we all face particular insecurities. Even when they have nothing to do with the job or specific project, they can still affect the team. Fear, lack of confidence, anxiety, and defensiveness are all signs that someone is feeling insecure.

A few years ago I began hosting a three-day intensive workshop on how to improve your speaking skills and find your speaking voice. I launched the Butterworth Communicators Institute in 2004 in order to help men and women feel more comfortable with their unique speaking style.

But as you can imagine, public speaking is accompanied by its archnemesis—fear. In every workshop, I encounter at least one attendee with serious fears about speaking in public. In the seminar, as I explore the fear of public speaking, I present the traditional approaches that have been used throughout the years. But more and more we are discovering that folks are afraid because they are struggling with a deeper, broader issue: personal insecurity.

When Sam came to BCI, the thought of standing to give his name and occupation almost paralyzed him. He made it through the introductory speech, but he was ready to go home after the first day. He waited for the other conferees to leave the room so he could tell me his decision. "I think I made a mistake coming here," he confessed. "It is no reflection on you or your teaching. This is a wonderful seminar. It's just not for me."

"Can we talk about it?" I asked.

"Sure, but I don't have much to say," he replied.

As we talked about his situation, his job, his home life, it became clear to me that Sam was fighting an uphill battle just to get out of bed in the morning. So many issues plagued him that it was not surprising to see why he felt panic when asked to speak in front of a group.

"As I listen to your life's story," I began gently, "it almost sounds as if you are afraid to speak publicly because you don't want anyone to get a glimpse into your real life."

Before I could say more, Sam's eyes welled up with tears.

As we discussed his situation in greater detail, we came up with a plan to make the three-day seminar bearable. We would speak only about "safe" subjects, ones that did not require Sam to divulge more information than he was ready to share. But the long-term plan I suggested to Sam included someone more qualified than a speech coach to help him overcome his insecurities. Sam agreed that he should see a counselor to get to the bottom of his issues.

As Sam's story illustrates, we may not even be aware of the personal insecurities that are holding us back in our careers. Sam felt that his lack of public speaking skills was a prime reason he was constantly passed over for promotions, but as I spoke with him, I realized that fear of public speaking was only a symptom of deeper unresolved issues.

Fear—it can cripple us if we're not careful. Sam's story, though wrapped around the fear of speaking in public, illustrates how our personal insecurities can get in the way of our success in life. Who wants to be on a team with a co-worker best described as "high maintenance"? The optimal plan is a team made up of people who are working through their own insecurities, therefore freeing them up to give their best to the team.

WHICH CAME FIRST—THE CHICKEN OR THE SILLY PUTTY?

Back when I was in graduate school, one of the classes I took that affected me the most profoundly was entitled Concepts of Self.

Although my areas of specialty were administration and supervision, I found myself taking a fair number of psychology classes, and this was one of them.

We studied all the great psychological theorists, people who contributed volumes of information on how people feel about themselves. What constitutes a self-image? Is it the way you feel about yourself? Is it the way others feel about you? Is it the way you think others feel about you? These are the sorts of issues that drove our study one semester.

For one assignment, we were each given a particular theorist whom we were to research. Then we had to write a report on the person for the professor and orally present to the class a summary of what this person had said about how we think about ourselves, how self-esteem is established, and what its implications are for our lives. That sort of assignment was fairly predictable. After about four presentations, the rest of the class was either sound asleep or completely confused.

But the professor redeemed himself later in the semester by assigning us another project. Putting a creative spin on the traditional term paper, he asked us to answer the question "How do *you* see self-image demonstrated in our world today?" It was the creative side of the assignment that has stuck with me all these years.

I came up with a three-part visual aid to explain self-image, using three objects to represent the different parts of the process we go through in determining how we feel about ourselves. The first object was a golf-ball-size plastic chicken that I stole from one of my kids' Fisher-Price barnyard set. I used the chicken to represent *our goals—our ideal self.* (Stay with me here; I know it sounds bizarre.) The chicken represented the ultimate in our lives, the realization of fulfilling all that we can be.

The next item I used was a plastic, life-size egg. Do you remember Silly Putty? It comes in an egg exactly like the one I am describing. In my project the egg represented *the self we project to others—our public self.* This is the self I have carefully crafted in order to safely show others who I am. Notice I use the word *safely.* The real me may be completely different, hidden beneath layers of protection. All I show the world is the me I want others to see. The rest I guard like Fort Knox.

The final item in my project was the Silly Putty itself. For those who don't know what Silly Putty is, it is a small, claylike glob of...putty. It is moldable, pliable, and lots of fun on a boring day. As kids, we used to put it on a frame of our comic books and press it down. When we took it off, it had copied the color picture from the comic book onto itself. The Silly Putty represented *my real self—my private self.* It may never be seen by anyone but me, yet it constitutes how I truly view myself. I may appear cool and confident to others around me, for example, but deep down inside I may be one scared puppy.

As I made my oral presentation, I sought to bring all three objects together. Obviously, the chicken is the ideal mature developmental stage of an egg. I want to grow, learn, and mature to achieve my ultimate potential. The egg is the protective shell I use to guard me from being too exposed and vulnerable so that I don't get hurt. And the Silly Putty is the real me. It's moldable and pliable, meaning I can shape my self-image however I want. It is what's inside an egg that grows up to become the chicken!

Your team—whether it's your group, your division, your company—is full of these putty-filled eggs. You may have team members who portray an air of well-educated, highly trained self-confidence and aplomb (the egg) when in reality they are scared little boys or girls (the putty). And if you don't do anything to overcome it, that personal insecurity can deep-six a team, robbing it of its effectiveness.

Few of us are trained therapists, so dealing with this can be tricky. If you sense a fair amount of personal insecurity on your team, and if it seems to be coming from one or two particular team members, bringing in a professional (for example, a therapist or an organizational psychologist) for a few sessions may be one way to go. But in many instances, people just need to know they are on equal footing, and with open, honest communication based on a healthy respect for one another, the effectiveness of the team can be greatly improved.

Another way to combat insecurity in team leaders, as well as in team members, is to differentiate between acceptance and approval. The nature of our jobs requires us to offer and receive approval—for example, ensuring an assigned task was completed well rather than poorly. Approval is based on performance. Acceptance, on the other hand, is based on personal worth. A wise team leader communicates unconditional acceptance of each team member *regardless* of performance. Being accepted for who we are naturally frees us up to work more diligently on the task at hand.

Becoming *friends* with the people on your team can go a long way in this regard. I know there is a lot of discussion on whether bosses should be friends with their employees, and certainly there is a danger here. A boss who becomes too close with team members can lose his or her professional respect. Personal friendship can create a situation where team members overstep their boundaries and use their advantage for selfish ends. And unfortunately, some team leaders need to exercise more authority and retain a level of managerial distance. But by and large, this is not the case. Over the years I have seen several examples of men and women who befriended some of their subordinates, and it did wonders for the productivity and effectiveness of the team.

If we can put our personal insecurities on the shelf for the good of the team, the team will actually help us deal with some of them! I know that sounds pretty amazing and almost backward, but I have seen it work dozens of times.

Three

The Barrier of Unhealthy Competition

Most business literature will tell you that one of the keys to success in the marketplace is competition. But while there are many positive aspects of a competitive environment, there are also dangers to consider.

One of the greatest dangers brought on by competition is the misperception that we are competing against fellow team members. On a team, it is absolutely vital to remember that *everyone on the team must win!* If we are competing for any other purpose, we are going to capsize the effectiveness of the team.

Sure, the nature of business includes competition. As you and your co-workers climb your way up the corporate ladder, there will be numerous occasions when several of you compete for just one spot. But there is a difference between healthy and unhealthy competition, as I discovered in the case of Al and Rose.

Al and Rose worked at the same company, at the same level

on the organizational chart. As sales managers for two different territories in the United States, they not only paid close attention to how their salespeople functioned, but they paid equally close attention to the positions above them.

So when the vice president of sales indicated that she might be moving into a different position, Rose and Al knew instinctively that the two of them had a chance to land the promotion to the VP post. Their new motivation caused their respective sales forces to kick it up a couple of notches. The result was a record sales quarter for both of them—and subsequent promotions as well. Rose got the brass ring. She was promoted to VP of sales. Al, however, was not overlooked. He remained a sales manager but was given a larger territory, which translated into a substantial raise. That's healthy competition where everyone wins.

Unhealthy competition is where things get out of hand. Infighting, personal insecurities, gossip, and lack of camaraderie overtake an efficiently functioning team and quickly turn it sour.

It is possible, however, to have interteam rivalry. If the northern office wants to challenge the southern office to a sales contest for the second quarter, it can be done in such a way that the competition is a positive motivator for the whole team.

Since I often speak to professional athletes, I gravitate toward putting these thoughts into sports terms. Let's suppose you are a star athlete on one of the thirty-two teams in the National Football League. You are breathing rarified air—so few of your peers at the college level were able to make the leap from the NCAA to the NFL. But you also know the job won't remain yours if you don't put in the hard work necessary to maintain your place on the team's roster. That's where competition enters the picture. You work, and you work hard. The competition from your teammates keeps you on your toes, at the top of your game—you work hard to maintain the role of starter. This is healthy competition. Teammates challenge one another and motivate one another to be the best they can be.

However, it is important to point out that competition can go afoul if it springs from a motive of selfishness. Competing only because "it's all about you" is not the sort of attitude that breeds teamwork.

Here's the easiest way to get your arms around what I'm saying. Your goal in competition should be the Super Bowl, not the Pro Bowl. The Pro Bowl is the NFL's version of the All-Star Game, honoring personal achievement at each individual position. The Super Bowl, on the other hand, is not about personal excellence as much as it is victory for the team. We've all seen moments in sports where a player forgoes a personal best in deference to what's better for the team, but we might not realize that we can make the same kind of heroic sacrifices for the good of our teams at work. Looking out only for yourself leads to selfish competition, and that is as unhealthy for a team as smoking three packs a day.

I'm going to give you an example of unhealthy competition in the workplace, and then I'm going to tell you about a group that is doing it right.

Sandra confided in me when she hired me to speak to her

group of insurance executives. "We've got a little situation here," she said, "and I am hoping you can address it in order to bring some relief."

"What's going on?" I asked.

"Well, we've got a company full of hard-charging folks who want to succeed at any price," she began.

"Sounds like it can get pretty cutthroat."

"Yes—and that is precisely the problem. Let me explain. Our men and women tend to specialize in selling a particular type of insurance. One person may be a life insurance specialist; another handles health insurance. Overall we have a wonderful success rate in using this model, but lately we've uncovered a disturbing situation."

"Go on," I prodded.

"I'll bottom line it for you." She sighed. "We encourage a lot of in-house competition, and that has usually been a good thing. But if Bob is selling auto insurance to a client and the client expresses interest in medical insurance, the natural thing to do would be to refer him down the hall to Cindy, right? But Bob doesn't want to get behind in competing against Cindy, *so he will refer the client to our competitor!* That way he assures himself that he hasn't contributed to Cindy's success and the possibility that she could sell more in this business quarter than he has."

It was clear the in-house competition had gotten out of hand. As we talked in more detail, I suggested that a heart-to-heart talk was in order for all involved. Unfortunately, the competitive juices were so high within the company that they had abandoned their formerly healthy business model. The bottom line took a hit, and if you ask me, unhealthy competition was the culprit.

But let me share a story from the good side of business practices.

I have a dear friend in Boston named Richard Catarano. Rich and his partner, Dick Vitale (the accountant, not the basketball commentator), run an extremely successful firm of certified public accountants. With more than three hundred people in their firm, they are setting new industry standards for how to run a business.

One of the creative ideas these guys have put together is an "All-Firm Day" two or three times each year. They have meals together, have fun together, and get to know one another with "Up Close and Personal" segments throughout the day. A portion of the day is given over to business, but the majority of the day is handed to an outside-the-firm motivational speaker like me, who is asked to instruct the group on issues relating to personal growth—things like balancing work and life, managing change, and learning to work as a team.

There is something about this kind of camaraderie in the midst of competition that inspires quality teamwork. Everyone I talked to in more personal and private settings loved working at this firm. They thought their bosses were incredible, because management genuinely cared about them. Work was not about competing, even though there was plenty of competition in the firm. It was about everyone being part of the same team.

Trust me, this firm delivers the goods! They see the danger in unhealthy competition that can undermine their efforts. So they band together, assisting one another wherever they can, and a quality product is the result. Their clients are satisfied, and as a result, they stay with the firm. I know Rich is probably blushing as he reads these words, and he would be the first one to say their firm is far from perfect. But they are an excellent example of teamwork and its by-product: success.

Four

The Barrier of Noncommunication

One of the most common struggles all teams face is the inability to communicate effectively. Stan knows what he wants Todd to accomplish, but because he can't correctly communicate the order to Todd, Stan is one frustrated partner. It's like a quarterback in a huddle suddenly being struck with an inability to speak English. He wants to call the play, but all that comes out of his mouth is French. If he's lucky, there may be a player or two who spent a couple of seasons with NFL Europe, but chances are, most of his team will have no idea whether they're running, passing, kicking, or punting.

Or let's use an illustration even closer to home—home. Many who read these pages are part of an elite team, specially chosen to create maximum effectiveness. In our culture, we refer to it as marriage. Many marriages suffer from the barrier of noncommunication. Granted, some couples just don't talk. But in other couples, one spouse *speaks,* and the other *listens* (the two key words in communication, right?), yet there is still no communication. What causes this?

Consider this slice of life from a young married couple. Brad and Shawna have been married for five years. They are both hardworking, upwardly mobile, success-oriented people. Brad works as a creative director in an advertising agency. Shawna manages a chain of stores.

On one particular day, Shawna has arranged to have the day off. She has an idea she has been working on for a month. After recently finishing a night class in gourmet cooking, Shawna has decided to surprise Brad with a gourmet meal made entirely from scratch as the prelude to an evening of love and romance.

Shawna's day is spent shopping at several grocery stores and specialty shops for just the right ingredients. At home, the lengthy process of cooking begins. All the burners on the stove are in use at the same time, and Shawna places yet another dish in the oven as the microwave timer goes off. She is determined to make this one incredible meal! She is very organized and extremely gifted at scheduling and timing. She is able to put this amazing meal together by early afternoon and still have time to take a relaxing bath before Brad arrives home. Perusing her closet, she chooses an outfit that says, "This is intended as a very romantic evening for just the two of us." A baby-sitter picks up little Tyler from day care and takes him to the playground and then to Brad's parents' house for the evening.

Now let's take a peek at Brad's day. It was horrible! From the time he arrives at the office, it is one thing after another, all piling up into a tower of stress. The morning begins with news from his supervisor that the Franklin Jewelry account pushed up its due date a full month, meaning the final sketches Brad was working on are due in final form right away. Brad thought he had another two weeks to work on this project!

What he thought would be a diversionary lunch from his troubles just adds to them. David, Brad's right-hand man for the last three years, takes him to lunch to tell him that he is accepting a position at a rival firm across town.

"What am I going to do without you?" Brad asks his friend and co-worker.

"You'll do just fine," David responds, but both of them know that "fine" will take many months to achieve.

Back in the office, Brad is met with a phone message saying that the Harding and Monroe Winery has called a meeting of their marketing folks to reexamine the ad campaign set up by Brad. Even though they signed off on it, they are now having "serious reservations" about the effectiveness of the campaign, especially the print ads. Brad has received these phone calls before—he knows what they mean. He will be asked by his boss to completely redesign the Harding and Monroe campaign. Weeks of work down the drain like a bad pinot noir. The stress is mounting.

By the time Brad jumps into his car to drive home for dinner, he is completely wrung out physically and emotionally. It has been a bad day, and his mood reflects this. His only desire is to get through dinner with a minimal amount of damage, then plop in front of the TV and try to unwind.

Meanwhile, Shawna knows Brad will be home any minute. She lights candles and dims lights. The gourmet dinner is ready. It's a moment she has been dreaming about for a month.

Brad pulls into the driveway, parks the car, takes one last deep breath, and walks to the front door. As he opens it, his stomach muscles tighten and he braces himself. He is used to being "attacked" by a preschooler full of precocious energy and wearing hard shoes. Imagine his surprise when he walks into the entryway undisturbed. As he adjusts to that, he realizes the lights are off and the house is lit only by candles. Before he can completely process that information, the beautiful woman that is his wife, dressed in a gorgeous outfit, walks slowly down the hall, looking at him with love. She gives him a hug and kiss. Feeling like he is in a movie, Brad frantically tries to adjust his mood.

"Hi, sweetheart," Shawna whispers in Brad's ear. "Come to the dining room. I've made you something special."

Brad obediently follows his wife to the dining room. She seats him, places his napkin on his lap, and tells him to wait for one minute. She walks into the kitchen and picks up the gourmet dinner arranged on a beautiful tray. Shawna makes her entrance. "I've prepared a little something I think you're going to like," she coos.

"Beef stroganoff?" Brad asks.

"No, baby. A new dish. Something I've never made before. You may not have tasted anything like it."

Brad feels his mood darken again. He knows where this is going; he's been here before. She has made a new dish, he has no idea what to expect, and he will be required to give a glowing report.

Brad is especially on edge because he feels like the deck is stacked against him. His brain is reduced to the use of his five senses, but the lights are so low he cannot see what he will be eating. Just as he is pondering this, Shawna says to him, "Just relax tonight, my love. No work necessary on your part."

"What do you mean?" Brad asks, trying not to frown. *Please let this be over soon,* he thinks. *I just want to watch the game and unwind.*

"I'm going to feed you. Sit back and enjoy."

Great, Brad thinks. *Now I can't even guess what I'm eating. Is it hot or cold? Is Shawna going to cut it, stab it, or scoop it?*

A second later Shawna has already placed a portion of food inside Brad's mouth. He chews with fabricated enthusiasm and has barely swallowed before Shawna asks, "So, honey, how do you like it?"

Brad is in a whirlwind of emotions, searching for the right vocabulary choices. He hasn't had enough time to think about his answer to that question, but it requires an immediate response. Marshaling his thoughts, he finally says, "It's nice."

His pronouncement is met with an awkward silence. Brad

knows this does not bode well for him. He tries to think of something else to say, but Shawna speaks before he has a chance.

"Nice? *Nice?*"

Brad blinks.

"I've been in the kitchen all day preparing a one-of-a-kind gourmet meal from scratch, and all you can say is 'nice'?"

At this point, Shawna begins to blow out the candles and turn on the lights as she angrily marches around the house. So much for romance. It ain't gonna happen tonight.

By now Brad has had an opportunity to collect his thoughts. *What's wrong with "nice"?* he thinks. *"Nice," as opposed to "not nice" or "gross" or "could gag a maggot." I think "nice" is a pretty fair description.*

But Shawna, having spent hours preparing this meal, wanted something more along the lines of "Great!" "Unbelievable!" "One of the ten best meals in culinary history!" "Nice" doesn't measure up in this circumstance.

So what's going on here? In the memorable words from the movie *Cool Hand Luke,* "What we've got here is a failure to communicate!"

Let's examine why.

To do so, we need to diagram the process of communication. I know this may sound pedantic, but trust me. If you want to establish an effective team, you've got to nail communication to the floor.

First, we have the two people communicating in a way communications experts would call "linear communication." They would call Shawna and Brad the *sender* and the *receiver.* What that means is that one person does all the talking (sender) and the other person does all the listening (receiver). It looks like this:

SENDER → RECEIVER

The more effective option is called "circular communication," in which each person, in effect, switches roles, acting as both sender and receiver. It looks like this:

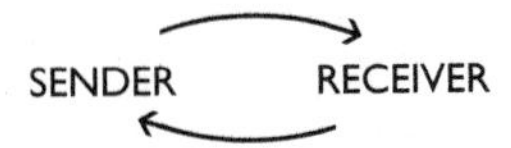

Instead of our communication being represented by an arrow, let's give it a name. Experts refer to it as the *signal.* It looks like this:

SENDER → (SIGNAL) → RECEIVER

In our story of Brad and Shawna, the signal was encapsulated in the word *nice.* But as I went into detail to describe, Brad had to search desperately for the best word to use to describe the meal. For many of us, this process is instantaneous, but it is still a process. It is referred to as *encoding,* which means putting our thoughts into words or some other form of communication. We add it to our diagram like this:

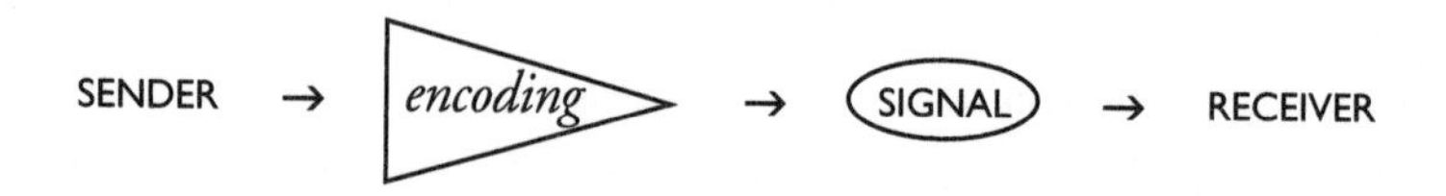

Of course, Shawna had to process the word *nice* in her mind as well, and she didn't care for Brad's word choice. This is called *decoding,* putting meaning to the signal that has been sent. It gets added to the diagram this way:

Now, that alone is a handsome diagram, but the key element is still missing. Why did Brad choose the word *nice*? Remember how he contrasted it to other, less complimentary words? What was behind all these mental calisthenics? Well, once again, it explains in painful detail how this tale of woe came about. Stated simply, Brad had a bad day! That was the starting point for the exchange. So what we need to do to our diagram to indicate that is to place an oval around three words: *sender, encoding,* and *signal.* Communication experts call this oval our *field of experience.*

FIELD OF EXPERIENCE

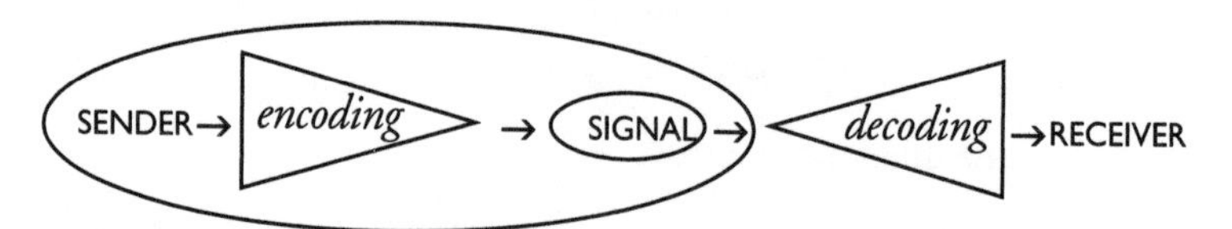

What about Shawna? She had a full day of hard work also and expectations of a great deal more enthusiasm from Brad. Her frame of reference, or field of experience, comes into play as well.

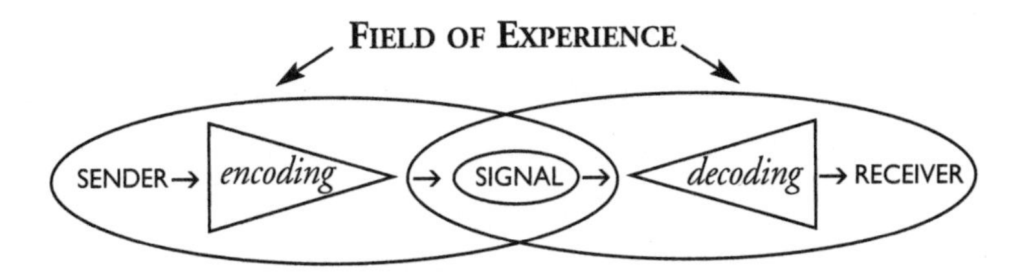

That's our completed diagram.[1] Do you see how this diagram gets to the bottom of how our everyday conversations break down? We talk to one another, but we do not take into account the other person's field of experience or frame of reference. Or as we used to say in the sixties, "Where's your head at, man?" If we are going to be effective in communicating with our teammates, whether at home or in the office, we have to go the extra mile and seek to discover their world.

There's a reason your normally even-tempered co-worker seems a little testy these days. There may be a situation at home or in another area of his life that feels like a volcano erupting. He may be trying to act professional at work, but the pressure from other areas can creep in, subtly or not so subtly. It explains why your boss, who has built her team around friendly, gregarious relationships, is now barking at you. She is getting barked at from her boss, and he is not backing down. No wonder she is making your life so miserable. But you wouldn't understand either of those scenarios if you didn't know the context of their lives. Of course we cannot know every nuance of one another's lives, but the more we do know, the more effective we can be in our communication. And the more effective we are in our communication, the more successful our team will be!

One way to get to the heart of communication issues, whether it be with a spouse or a boss or a co-worker, is to ask the simple question, "So how's it going?" Of course, this is likely to be answered with "Fine." So we have to dig a little deeper. "No, I really mean it. How are things going?" If we can get to the place with people where they feel comfortable enough to honestly share about their lives, we are given a window into their world. For instance, if there is a troubling situation in a person's life and he reveals it to you, it will clue you that he may have additional struggles with the task at hand. It's a risk, to be sure. But it's a risk that is worth it.

Another helpful element in communication is paraphrasing. When a team member speaks to you, tell him or her what you are hearing as it is being said. So many communication detours could be avoided if we took the time to really listen to what was being said and then made sure the end result was mutual understanding.

Team Tip:

A team can only be as good as the strengths of its relationships.

Five

The Barrier of Being Afraid to Change

The process of working through these barriers to effective teamwork includes mastering a few key skills. None is more important than managing change. Most of us don't handle change well, in general, so when it occurs as a result of becoming part of a team, it can be a major disruption. But if we understand how change works, figure out why we are frightened by it, learn how to deal with it, and put it in the proper perspective, we can stare down those negative issues and emerge the victor!

We are in a far better place if we choose to accept change, since it happens to us whether we choose to accept it or not. Making friends with change can revolutionize our lives, not only by facilitating teamwork, but also by giving us tools for handling all kinds of life issues.

THE PROCESS OF CHANGE

When I speak in the corporate world, I am often asked to address the topic of change. Early in the presentation I ask the audience to visualize a flow chart of life. Using eight words that begin with the letter C, I walk them through a typical passage in our lives.

I always begin with *calm.* Most of us like the sound of that word, and it starts us off on our journey in a positive way. We like days that are orderly and scheduled, as opposed to days of upheaval.

We are calm when it seems that life is under our *control.* Things just work out better when they are done the way we like them done. Control is a good thing, and the more of life that is under our control, the happier we tend to be.

But then it happens. We are faced with a fork in the road, and neither direction looks inviting. One side of the fork is a *crisis;* the other side of the fork is a *choice.* Both of these directions lead somewhere we don't want to go—*change.* I can choose to change, or I can wait for change to come upon me, but either way, an out-of-control part of life has produced something new that I would rather resist—a change.

But change can bring about some wonderful results if we are willing to follow it through. Change can produce *confidence.* We can learn valuable lessons from change and consequently become better people for it.

When we build confidence, it shows, but often it means we

have deepened our *character* on the inside, as well. Who hasn't been inspired by a book, movie, or television show about someone who was dealt a difficult blow in life yet learned to fight back and so emerged stronger than before? Change isn't always bad. Sometimes it can have a very positive influence in our lives.

And once we've accepted change and learned from it, we are brought back to *calm*. Life returns to normal, if only for a little while.

Think about this flow chart and your current status on your team. Now imagine what would happen if a change occurred today. Let's say all was calm when you showed up for work this morning—or at least that was the appearance you liked to present. Life was good because every aspect seemed under your control. But then something happened, leading to change. Maybe it was something you chose, like delegating part of your responsibilities to the new member of the team, or maybe something was forced upon you, like being asked to work with a difficult colleague. Whether it was a choice or a crisis, a radical change took place.

As traumatic as it might seem at the time, if you use change as an opportunity to learn and grow, you will gain a sense of confidence and deepen your character. Don't dwell on the first part of the chart. We've all been there. It's happened, and it's time to move on. Focus on the latter part of the chart: what you can do to turn change into a positive force in your life. That sounds pretty good, doesn't it?

But it's still scary, isn't it?

WHY CHANGE FRIGHTENS US

When most of us think about change, we experience something of a jolt in our stomach. For some of us, it might be a little stomach churning; for others, it can feel as if we just swallowed an entire ocean. Either way, change can be frightening, even painful.[2] Why?

Change brings out the *fear of the unknown.* We find ourselves thinking, *Better to fight the devil I know than the one I don't!* As horrible as those last few weeks or months might have been prior to the changes on the team, at least we knew what to expect. It's not knowing what's ahead that can be maddening. We like control, and any change will seem to throw everything out of our hands. We liked our life better when we were in charge, but for the moment those days are gone. Things have changed, and that drives us crazy.

Another reason change frightens us is the *fear of failure.* No one likes to fail. Being forced to change raises a question we don't like to consider: what if this change causes me to fall flat on my face? We know we can work on the team as it was, but what if we can't handle the responsibilities? If we fail—it's just too embarrassing to think about! And it's exactly that kind of thinking that keeps us from the positive changes we need to make for the good of the team.

Fear of commitment is another reason change frightens us. Changes force us to ask, "What do I really want?" We might say we want to learn and grow from this experience, but do we mean it? Are we committed to our team enough that we will work through the process, learning all the lessons intended for us along the way? This kind of change forces us to identify our values, and that can be a daunting task.

Some of us are afraid of change because of a *fear of disapproval.* If we take on a new role previously assigned to another team member, we risk people saying that they liked things better the way they were, that they liked us better the way we were before. Those of us who have handled difficult or negative changes in our lives know this feeling well. "I liked it better when you were an assistant" or "...when Jane was in charge" or whatever. Most people don't say it, but it's there; we can feel it in the air. People treated us better before the team dynamics shifted, we convince ourselves, and suddenly we are back to square one, shouldering a boatload of self-esteem issues.

For some of us, the strongest fear regarding change is the *fear of success.* That may sound a little strange, but sometimes the most paralyzing thought is that success will bring with it a host of changes for which we may not be ready. So instead, we self-destruct, unconsciously sabotaging our own plan.

"I guess it's a normal reaction," Randall confided in me after I had made a presentation to his employer.

"What are you talking about?" I asked.

"Our company recently merged with another company here in town. Actually it was more like a hostile takeover than a merger. They combined the workforces by choosing the best person from either company for each individual position. Consequently, our

IT department was a brand-new team—three guys from my original company and three from the other company.

"Frankly, I was angry at the change. I missed having a couple of my people in the key slots. Something inside of me just wanted to have it back the way it was."

"So what happened?" I pressed him.

"Well, eventually we congealed into an effective team. But early on, it was like I wanted our team to fail so we could get the old team back together again. I guess that's what I meant when I said it was a normal reaction—not wanting a new team to succeed because you're still emotionally attached to the old one."

Maybe you identify with one of the reasons we fear change. Maybe you identify with quite a few of them. Some of these fears will manifest themselves in a fairly straightforward way and will be easy to identify. But some of us may need help in this process. Fear of change is a blind spot for many people, and the only way to get a blind spot out in the open is to ask those around us to help us see what we're missing. Jot down the names of two or three close friends or co-workers and, perhaps over a cup of coffee, review these five fears of change with them. Ask them if any of these fears are working in your life without your knowing it. What happens as a result could be significant both to you and your team.

The issue boils down to this: what can we do to make change our friend? There are several steps we can take. They involve being more goal oriented, taking a little more command, and making more positive choices.

BEFRIENDING CHANGE IN OUR LIVES

What can you do to begin moving closer to your ultimate goals as a team?

Have your team members start with small, specific, limited goals in areas where you want change. This sounds basic, but it is where many of us get tripped up—at the outset. We decide we want to change, but we make our goals so grand that they are unattainable.

The best way to approach change is to make a small addition to your daily routine. Suppose your team at work has just been handed a new assignment that's pretty large in scope. The wise team leader, assuming the schedule allows for this strategy, will introduce small tasks gradually as opposed to "dumping the whole truckload" at once. The team won't feel so overwhelmed, and the emotional strain will be kept to a minimum. But over time, the complete change will be made.

Proactive change will always be easier than reactive change. I've alluded to this point the entire chapter, so let's get it down in black and white. Change we can control will always be easier to handle than change that is forced upon us. If we knew a hurricane or a tornado was headed for our homes, it would be easier to make the choice to leave with some belongings rather than wait for the winds and rain to hit.

Choosing to change on our own terms is also easier to handle emotionally—it doesn't create as much imbalance, and we recover much faster. Why? Because we have control. We are deciding our circumstances, not waiting around for them to hit us in the face.

For example, if a change in our personal lives has affected our work performance on our teams, we have a choice ahead of us. Either we choose to get ourselves in gear and return to the quality work we were known for in the past, or we choose to wait around for the pink slips. Or maybe we go to our boss and explain that we are dealing with something difficult at home. Maybe we take a little time off to get things in order. Ask yourself, how can I change a potentially flawed aspect of our team, or my ability to function on the team, *before* that problem *forces* me to change?

Choose to stretch yourself. This is all about risk. Some of us respond favorably to risk, but the rest of us are scared.

Several years ago I realized I had combed my hair the same way for decades. When parted down the left side, it fell into place naturally. Then my wife and some of my kids suggested I adopt a different hairstyle, a more contemporary one. I threw up all sorts of arguments: "I've always worn my hair this way! It was good enough for Abraham Lincoln! If I change my haircut, it would scream 'midlife crisis'!" But guess what happened? I tried it, and I liked it! People said I looked ten years younger (a good thing to say to someone my age). It doesn't take any time to comb; it's almost like the crew cut I got every summer as a child.

A new hairstyle was a stretch for me. It was thinking way outside the box for an I've-always-done-it-this-way kind of guy. But now that I've done it, I'm so glad I did. And if it works that way with hair, think about your team and your life!

A friend of mine who runs a small manufacturing company often chuckles over a time several years ago when he was faced with an opportunity to stretch his team. "We became aware of some brand-new, state-of-the-art technology that would increase our productivity by 20 percent. Of course, the price tag on this technology was astronomical. I did a little research and discovered none of my competitors were using this stuff. So the safe, easy, and cheap route would have been to maintain the status quo.

"Fortunately we didn't do that. We bit the bullet, bought hundreds of thousands of dollars worth of equipment, and before you know it, we were the leader in our industry. Now, of course, *all* my competitors use this technology. So ultimately, we would have gotten on board as well. But because we chose to stretch ourselves, we were, and still are, the lead dog!"

So go ahead, take a risk, even a small one. Stretch yourself.

Take care of yourself. Part of teamwork is taking good care of yourself. Some of us address our pain by pouring our lives into helping someone else. Taking care of another person distracts us from the work we need to be doing in our own lives, especially in times of difficulty. So, even though it sounds noble to help out a brother, don't allow your concern for others to get in the way of your own healing.

It reminds me of the preflight announcements that our "on-the-fly" friends, the flight attendants, make: "Put your oxygen mask on first before helping others." Do you balance pleasing others with taking care of yourself? It's important to work on your own behalf, as well. It's the right thing to do.

Here's an exercise to help you assess your team's ability to befriend change. Ask yourself the following questions and answer as honestly as you can:

- How important are calm and control to my team?
- Do we tend to create change or wait until it's dumped on us?
- How much is the fear of the unknown playing into our reluctance to change?
- Are we more afraid of failure or of success when it comes to change?
- Proactive change will always be easier than reactive change. What do I need to do to get my team to buy into that concept?
- What are some specific things we could put in motion to get our team to befriend change?

Part Two

The Great Traits of Effective Teams

Six

Respect: We Are like a Family

We are now ready to look at the great traits of effective teams. The rest of this book will concentrate on identifying characteristics of successful groups. You may think some of these traits are obvious, but don't be too hasty and just skim through them. There is much worth considering here, even in the "simple" stuff. These characteristics seem obvious because lots of teams have used them through the years to become successful.

An explanatory metaphor—a family, an athletic team, or a choir and an orchestra—will attend each trait. This is done to fulfill a simple law of learning: *abstract concepts are best learned through the use of concrete symbols.* You may forget the principle of respect in a few days, but my hope is you will always remember the family story that illustrates it.

Team Tip:

Every team member is different.

Treat each person with respect.

THE FAMILY TEAM

When I think of respect, I think of a family. A family is a beautiful metaphor for the way a team can work effectively toward a common goal and yet, at the same time, recognize and celebrate each individual member. Think about your family. Each member is different, and it is those differences that make each of them the individual you love and respect.

For example, all five of my kids looked *exactly alike* when they were born (at least to me they did). Really. They looked like quintuplets, they were so alike. Each of them had a wonderfully full, round face with squeezable cheeks. Add a tiny patch of soft, white-blond hair, and you had my five little towheads.

It was at this point that I made a huge mistake. Following what I believed to be a logical pattern, I assumed that since they *looked* alike, they would *act* alike.

Nothing could have been further from the truth.

I conducted my fathering with that mistruth as my motto for quite a few years until I finally woke up and began observing the way my kids took to different activities in their young lives:

I have children who are incredibly athletic.

I have children who are marvelously gifted musicians.

I have children who love art and excel in it.

I have children who are intellectual,

...and I have children who aren't.

So, even though they may look alike and bear the same last name, there is great diversity in our family. And even though we are all very different, we must still respect one another. All of us are vital and valued members of the family team.

Team Tip:

Make sure the entire team gets rewarded for victories and successes.

EACH MEMBER IS IMPORTANT

It is one thing to give lip service to the maxim that all team members are important and that their contribution is vital to our success. It is something quite different to give action to those words. Truly effective team members respect everyone on the team—from the top level to the bottom. And they consistently demonstrate that respect.

Mike Sime runs a company in Minneapolis called Creative Carton, and as he likes to put it, "I've got the best job in the world. I run a company that sells empty boxes!" I first met Mike at a Young Presidents' Organization meeting where I was speaking. We hit it off immediately. Mike is one of the kindest, most generous people I know. He exudes energy and goodwill, and he is one of the most charismatic leaders I have ever met. His business consistently makes a solid profit, and I believe he would tell you that part of his success stems from his commitment to teamwork.

A few years ago Mike invited me to speak at the company's annual Christmas party. His desire was to give his employees a reward for a big year. So instead of just feeding them a dinner and passing out a bonus in an envelope, he planned a giant party.

My wife and I were driven to a beautiful, upscale restaurant in the area on a cold and windy winter's night. Once inside the restaurant, however, an immediate feeling of warmth permeated the people gathered.

Mike and his lovely wife, Pam, gave the employees a fabulous dinner, complete with everything a gourmet could ask. After dinner, Mike introduced me, and I made my presentation. I was asked to speak on the topic of teamwork, and it quickly became apparent that I was preaching to the choir! My speech simply affirmed what they already were doing. The success of this company is based on the employees' ability to work together as an effective team.

Upon the conclusion of my remarks, Mike got up and fondly recalled the highs and lows of the previous year. The entire crowd lit up with the victories and nodded their heads at the recollection of the tough times. But watching Mike simply tell his teammates how important every one of them was to the company, how the bottom line of the good year reflected each person's contribution—well, it was a magical moment.

Just when I thought nothing could surpass this feeling of warmth and camaraderie, we began the annual passing out of the Christmas presents. Each person had been given a ticket upon entering the dining room. Mike now began reading numbers out loud as if he were awarding a door prize. "Number 384," Mike would announce, and an excited man or woman would hustle up to the stage to receive a present.

This is where it got really interesting. The winner could accept the prize he or she was given or could swap it for a prize already awarded to another. There were gifts for every taste and design. There were power tools, cookbooks, sporting goods, concert tickets, gift baskets, sporting event tickets, gift certificates for restaurants and hotels, and a host of other niceties.

The first gift to be awarded was an autographed jersey from a star Minnesota Vikings football player. There was a lot of laughter as person after person chose the autographed Vikings jersey. It was quite comical, since whoever chose it would immediately put it on over his party clothes to show how much he loved it and wanted to keep it. Then, when the next person selected the same prize, the previous winner would grimace and reluctantly give his teammate the shirt off his back!

But it was the *attitude* behind all this frivolity that made a mark on me and the rest of the room. This group of people loved each other. The party included the entire company, from top executives all the way through the organizational chart to the frontline workers. To see a forklift operator "steal" the jersey away from a vice president and the VP respond good-naturedly was a vivid picture of a company that honors its employees at all levels.

It's all about respect. Mike Sime understands the importance of sharing victories and successes with the entire team. The bond that is created during the good times will be helpful down the road, should the company deal with days of difficulty. Showing appreciation and respect to all his employees by including them in the celebration helps Mike express how much he values their contribution. In that way, he is an example to us all.

Team Tip:

Never forget: every job is an important job.

- What are you doing on your team to encourage respect among your teammates?
- Do you see your team as a family? How would you describe some of the "family members" on your current team? What strengths do they add to your family? What challenges do they bring with them? How can you turn their challenges into strengths?

Seven

Sacrifice: We Are like an Athletic Team

Of all the speaking assignments I've had, I can tell you without hesitation that my favorites have been the opportunities to speak to twenty-six of the thirty-two teams of the National Football League. I have the athletic ability of tile grout, but I am a huge fan. Hanging out with a team at their hotel for a couple of hours on game day still excites me.

Often NFL coaches bring in an outside speaker on game day to provide motivation and inspiration for the team from someone other than themselves. I work diligently to give an inspiring, humorous, and thought-provoking message in twenty to twenty-five minutes. Former head coach Don Shula once told me that I could speak as long as I wanted but that in half an hour the team would walk out to go to the pregame meal! But there is another incentive to giving brief, entertaining remarks. If the team likes your presentation, you are invited to join them at the pregame meal!

Usually the meal is served in the ballroom of the hotel where the team stays the night before the game. (Home teams usually stay at a hotel as well so the coaching staff can keep an eye on everybody.) On one occasion, however, the meeting was held in the basement, and the dining room was located on the first floor.

I spoke to the team, shook some hands, talked briefly with some of the players and coaches, and then headed down the hall to catch the elevator. "Hold that elevator!" I yelled as the doors began closing. They opened enough for me to jump in. It was at that point I discovered I had jumped on an elevator already filled with *eight offensive linemen.*

Trust me, these guys are huge!

The door closed, and the elevator labored for a few seconds before it came to an unscheduled stop between floors.

To my amazement all eight of these guys turned and glared at me. They started screaming, "Why did you get on this elevator?" They were convinced *I* was the reason the elevator was too heavy. Of course, I knew this was the only time in my adult life when I could be considered petite.

Seeing the panicked look on their faces, I realized I needed to divert their attention from the crisis. (I've never been able to ascertain if they were more afraid of missing the game or missing the meal.) I decided to ask them a question I had always wanted to ask a room full of offensive lineman. I didn't have an entire room, so an elevator would have to do. "Doesn't it ever bother you guys that you never get mentioned in the newspaper? Or let me rephrase it. Doesn't it bother you that you *only* get mentioned in the newspaper if you do something wrong? You know, miss a block, hike the ball over the kicker's head, stuff like that?"

My question not only effectively distracted them from death by elevator, but it also led to a deep insight into teamwork. "You don't understand, man," one replied. "Our job is not to get our names in the paper. Our job is to support the team so that the quarterback or the running back or the wide receiver gets into the paper. Our job is not about the glory. It's about helping the team win."

These guys had a firm grip on another important trait of effective teamwork: *sacrifice.*

Team Tip:

Sacrifice personal glory in order to support the team.

A key element on any sports team is *sacrifice.* You sacrifice personal glory for the good of the team. You sacrifice so you can be supportive to each member, thus preventing unhealthy competition. Any team runs better when it operates on the principle of sacrifice.

INTEGRITY IN YOUR BOX

An effective team is like a well-put-together sports organization. Each person understands his or her job and does it well while looking to help teammates in any way possible. This kind of attitude is born out of integrity, the strength of relationships with others on the team, and respect for each member's position. In other words, knowing the job and doing it well.

Andy Reid, head coach of the Philadelphia Eagles, knows the value of this principle. In an interview with the *Los Angeles Times,* he credited much of his team's success to that very notion.

> Myself, I take an offensive lineman's approach....
>
> Each guy doesn't have to be an all-star; they just have to be able to master their little [3 x 3] box on the field. Then you can master that big box which is the actual football field. You take that approach to it, you'll be OK.[3]

- So what's your three-by-three box on the team? Can you describe it in one sentence?
- How close are you to mastering your little box? Give yourself a grade, from an A+ all the way down to a failing grade of F.
- How can you improve your mastery of your box? List at least three practical strategies, one of which can be immediately implemented.

WORKS WELL WITH OTHERS

I am one of the many admirers of Tom Landry, the former coach of the Dallas Cowboys. Several years ago I helped Bill Bates, one of the Cowboys who played for Landry, write his autobiography. Bill allowed me unlimited access to his life, including offering to set up interviews for me with his parents, his high-school and college coaches, former and current teammates, and front-office personnel. I gave him my list of interview requests, with a two-hour visit with Tom Landry at the top.

Several weeks later I walked into Coach Landry's office and was met with a big surprise. Having viewed him only on television as he paced the sidelines, I always thought of him as fairly quiet, reserved, and stoic. That may have been true on the sidelines, but in his office I found him to be kind, warm, articulate, and quite funny.

We talked about Bill for a while, and he gave me some great information that became an important chapter in the book. When we finished, I noticed we still had time left in my two-hour appointment, so the two of us just sat back and swapped stories. We discovered some friends we had in common and talked about them for a while. He complimented me immensely by asking questions and being interested in my work. Eventually I asked him about his coaching style.

"I know I'm the coach who was known for the Xs and Os. I worked hard preparing each week's game plan. I wasn't the back-slapping motivator like many of my peers. But that doesn't mean I didn't understand the value of relationships. My players were very important to me."

Coach Landry gave me some valuable insight on the importance of personal connection with teammates, no matter what our personality may be. Many of us identify more with a Jimmy Johnson–type of head coach (the man who succeeded Tom Landry in coaching the Cowboys), who built a coaching career around the connection he had with his players. But Coach Landry's lesson is clear. Whether you are by nature outgoing and demonstrative or quiet and reserved, it is vital that you connect with those who make up your team.

In his book on success, Denver Broncos head coach Mike Shanahan talks about the value of relationships to the team's ultimate achievement of its goals. Teams matter more than individuals, he says.[4] It is important to value each member, share both victories and defeats, accept criticism, and keep the boss (the coach) well informed. That's what support looks like on an effective team, and support is born of sacrifice. You cannot build relationships within a team if you're focused solely on self-promotion.

- Name the three folks on your team you would call your closest co-workers.
- How would you describe your relationship with these three people?
- List two or three things you can do in the next two weeks to create a more personal connection with each of the co-workers you listed.

THE NFL, NOT THE PGA

Recently I was invited to give a presentation on teamwork to the Walt Disney Company. I used a number of analogies to make my point about teamwork: the Carnegie Hall story, the analogy of family, of the human body, and an athletic team. When the speech concluded, my friend and host, Mark Zoradi, president of Disney's Buena Vista Distribution, put the capstone on the event.

"Of all the analogies Bill used today, I was most taken by the analogy of an athletic team. That's exactly what we are here in the Disney family. Sure, we are a family, but we are more than that—we are a great athletic team. We are not competing against each other in a sport of individuals, but we compete *with* each other for the good of the team.

"To sum up my view of Bill's presentation, the bottom line is this: Don't think golf. Think football."

Whether you are the franchise player, the third-string lineman, the equipment manager, or the head coach, the same message applies: sacrifice your own glory so you can support one another.

- List three or four ways your team is like an athletic team.
- What position do you play on the team?
- Based on what you read in this chapter, can you think of three ways to create an atmosphere of mutual sacrifice and support on your team?

Eight

Creativity: We Are like a Choir and an Orchestra

Since I wasn't an athlete growing up, my parents thought it would be good to get me involved in the world of music. (Of course, back then, those were the only two options!) My mother sang in the church choir and even scored the occasional solo at Christmas or Easter. My dad played the alto saxophone in high school, dreaming of the day he would leave the streets of Philadelphia to tour with Glenn Miller and see the world, making sweet music.

So on a crisp, autumn Philadelphia morning, I sat with one other student in the chilly music room at our local elementary school as a nervous, sweaty fourth grader. Mr. Maio, the music teacher, made us feel like we were in the presence of royalty, not because he was in the room, but because of the elegant black cases on the table in front of us.

Each of those cases held our future—a brand-new clarinet.

I practiced faithfully on that licorice stick. I knew from talking to my classmates that it was much easier to play than most of the other instruments passed around the band room. Take the trumpet, for example. Figuring out how to make your lips vibrate was driving some of my classmates crazy. All I had to do to make a sound on the clarinet was blow into it. But it was still a challenge. If I could get my mouth properly positioned to create a sound, I couldn't get my fingers to play the notes, and when the fingers did what they were supposed to do, the mouth shut down. It was a struggle that accompanied me throughout my musical journey.

After three years of agony on the clarinet, I moved up to junior high school. The musical brain trust in junior high thought a new instrument might be the answer. So they presented me with the big brother to the clarinet, the alto saxophone. Their thinking was clear: the bigger the instrument, the easier time I would have mastering it. It was easier to blow into, but it did nothing to help my fumbling fingers. Another great idea, but it was not to be.

However, it was a good year from the vantage point that my dad was especially proud that I was following in his footsteps, playing the same instrument he had played. Of course, I sounded terrible on the thing, so I had to practice as soon as I got home from school each afternoon, before he came home from work. The less he heard me play, the prouder he was of me.

As seventh grade gave way to eighth grade, the "bigger is better" theory continued. Midyear I was called to the music office for yet another presentation. "Welcome to the world of the tenor sax!" my music teacher announced. "The alto sax's bigger brother." He regaled me with tales of Tex Beneke, Boots Randolph, and Junior Walker.

I gave it my best shot. I must admit, the blowing-into-the-instrument part of the equation was easier on the tenor sax. But the music was still challenging, and my fingers couldn't do the walking.

By the time I entered the ninth grade, it was a running joke how big a sax they'd need to make so that Butterworth could play it! Since the high school had more money in its music budget, I discovered there was at least one more move I could make.

The day I walked into the high-school band room to meet my new instrument was a bit jarring. The sax I was to play was still in its case, and the case was too large to sit on the table in front of me. The enormous blue box sat on the floor next to a folding chair. I opened the case to see the mother of all saxophones: the baritone sax.

Not only was it big, but it was heavy! As I strapped it around my neck, I tried to concentrate on the positives. *This will provide an excellent upper-body workout while I play it!* I thought. I was correct in my prediction. But the best news was that in our high school's musical collection there was hardly any music written for the baritone sax. What were they going to do with me? Thanks to a creative music teacher and a little transposing, I found my place in the band playing tuba parts.

I had entered the world of bum-bum, bum-bum, bum-bum. If you know anything about music, let me say it this way: quarter notes were my friends. I no longer had any need for the more difficult eighth notes or the especially tricky sixteenth notes. The solid undergirding of the tuba's quarter notes not only gave me a place in the band; it gave me a place where I could shine!

Those elementary, junior-high, and high-school days instilled in me a love for music. I loved the thrill of making music with other gifted (or more gifted, in my case) musicians. What I enjoyed most was how the notes on the page were repeated by each member of the band, yet each member had a unique, individual style that blended into a wonderful orchestral sound. As I look back on those rehearsals and performances, I can see the value the band director gave us by stressing our *creativity.*

And that creativity is important in your team as well, whether you know the difference between a sax and a bassoon or not! Creativity sparks good teams. It is essential for maximum performance. So how do you maximize creativity? By developing a style for your team that is more creative than predictable.

Accept the Challenge of Unexpected Opportunities

When I was in eighth grade (during my tenor-sax years of my saxophone evolution), a guitar player named Clint asked me if I wanted to join a rock band. The fact that Clint was a junior in high school made the offer flattering beyond refusal, and I became the fifth member of a garage band named the IV Romans. Bad math aside, it was a very educational experience for me. I don't want to say we sounded terrible, but to this day, it's the only time in my life I have ever been spit on. (It was during a concert—and that's all the detail I'm giving.)

It wasn't due to lack of rehearsing, as we practiced faithfully in Clint's family room. And it was during one of these rehearsals that I experienced an amazing phenomenon. We were learning a popular song of the day, "Hang On Sloopy." In the middle of the song, Clint yelled, "Take it, Bob!" and Bob began an improvised lead-guitar solo that would have made Eric Clapton proud. With no prior rehearsal and no advance planning, Bob allowed his creativity to express itself in a beautiful way.

After an appropriate amount of time, Bob's solo ended, and I smiled, overjoyed that we sounded so fine. That's when my world was rocked.

"Take it, Bill!" Clint screamed. My four bandmates looked at me.

They wanted *me* to improvise a solo.

I'd never had a solo before and frankly had no idea where to find one. But I knew what key we were in and what notes were acceptable, so I swallowed hard, took a deep breath, and began to play.

I started with a trill, which is where you alternate between two notes as fast as you can. As nervous as I was, I trilled at supersonic speed. It sounded good, it sounded right, and it bought me enough time to figure out what to do next. I went down the scale, hitting notes in rare form. I was actually improvising a solo! The other four IV Romans were very pleased, and I was quite impressed with myself.

My point is, this never would have happened if Clint hadn't provided me with the opportunity to express myself in my own way. Because he gave me that kind of freedom, I unleashed my creativity in a way that benefited all my teammates.

Nancy knows how this works in the business world. She oversees a team of seven people, who all report to her. On a regular basis she is responsible for presentations to other divisions of the company. Nancy speaks well, but her presentations have soared to new levels. Why?

"I have the best team!" she's quick to explain. "About three months ago, I was meeting with my team to prepare for a particular presentation. I discovered Vicky was brilliant at PowerPoint slides. She designed some for my talk, and, trust me, they were way better than I could've done myself. Another co-worker volunteered to help collect some case studies to balance out my facts and figures."

Nancy is my kind of leader. By keeping an eye out for unexpected opportunities, she gave each team member a chance to "solo" where they excelled, and as a result she built up the value of her entire team.

Look for Ways to Inspire and Motivate Your Team

Remember the story about Carnegie Hall at the beginning of this book? That experience is a rich illustration to me of all the different ways creativity can express itself. Sure, there are the obvious forms of creativity, those expressed by the conductor and the singers. You need sopranos and altos and tenors and basses to give each choral number its full sound. Break it down even further, and there are subtle differences between the first and second soprano, first and second tenor, and so on.

But there is more to that story about the value of creativity.

Once the conductor arrived onstage that evening, I was primed to notice all the parts of the symphonic equation that made up the sum of musical performances called a concert. I knew we needed all the singers and the conductor and the accompanist to give the full musical performance, but I sensed there was more. And I was correct.

I don't recall many of the numbers the conductor chose for the concert. I do remember there were classical pieces, modern pieces, pieces in English, pieces in Italian, challenging songs, and simple ones. It was one of the simple songs, "My Old Kentucky Home," that formed a lasting memory. As Stephen Foster's soulful melody unfolded in simple unison, the audience began to respond. Without any invitation or encouragement, people from the audience stood as the song progressed. Not the entire audience, just scattered members here and there. They seemed to be standing as couples—a man and woman on the third row, another couple on the twelfth.

Then I realized the couples who were standing were all parents of students from the great state of Kentucky. I later learned that when "My Old Kentucky Home" is sung in that state, people stand out of respect, much as we do for "The Star-Spangled Banner" across the nation.

Once again I was struck with the notion that every person is vital to the successful performance of a team. For example, there would have been no kids from Kentucky in this performance if moms and dads hadn't been doing more than singing "My Old Kentucky Home"—know what I mean? These parents were as much a part of the conductor's team as the students singing onstage were.

I was impressed by how the conductor chose pieces that would inspire both the choir and the audience. There was a palpable excitement in the air that evening. Through a variety of methods, including song choice, the conductor inspired his team, motivating them to perform in a way they would never forget.

LET GO OF IDEAS THAT ARE NOT WORKING

We'll leave Carnegie Hall for a bit but will return before the book's finale.

I first met Jim Franklin at a national conference for the Young

Presidents' Organization at which I was to present an after-dinner speech to kick off one of their always amazing meetings. As my wife, Kathi, conversed with Jim's wife, Ines, we soon discovered that we lived in the same part of the country—Southern California. As we talked, we realized that we lived close to one another. So we vowed to stay in touch after the conference concluded. A friendship began.

We began having dinner together as couples every few weeks, and I developed a better understanding of who the Franklins are and what their business is all about. HAR-BRO specializes in disaster relief through building restoration. If your house caught fire, for example, and the fire company rushed over and extinguished the blaze, you would still be left with lots of cleanup. HAR-BRO comes in and does things like drying carpets and putting plywood over broken windows and then restoring your home to its condition prior to the fire.

At one of our dinners, Jim asked me to speak to his company. "We tried something like this last year, and it seemed to go well," he explained. "We take some of our key people—about a hundred of them—and we go away for a full-day meeting. We talk about business issues, of course, but more important are the personal issues—how to deal with an ever-changing business and how to find balance in life. Can you speak to these issues?" I assured him I could offer input to his company on both of those topics and that it would be an enjoyable experience.

What Jim provided for his company I believe serves as an

excellent model for all businesses. He took his people off site to a beautiful country club. "Sure, it cost some bucks, but I wanted to send a message to my team that they are all very valuable to me," Jim said.

We met all morning, with a combination of my presentations, audience participation through small groups, large-group discussions, and team-building exercises that were fun and instructive at the same time. When noon rolled around, we were treated to a delicious buffet lunch and given some extra time to wander the grounds of the golf club. After lunch we focused our attention on balancing work and life. Everyone left the meeting at four feeling renewed and inspired.

Actually, we covered one more agenda item before we dismissed, and it is the reason I'm telling you this story. Jim passed out an evaluation form for the team to fill out. At first I thought this was a mere formality, but discussing it with Jim after the event gave me a new perspective on the evaluation. "Evaluations are critical to me in my business," he explained. "From all outward appearances, this day of meetings seems to be very helpful—a good use of funds. But if I discover from reading the evaluations that it is more of a day off than a learning experience, I have no problem pulling the plug on future events of this nature. You have to know when to let it go."

I've stayed in touch with Jim since that event, and every time I speak with him, he reminds me how wonderful that day was. "Our people loved it. The evaluations made it clear that it was time well spent." Of course, I am thrilled my part of the day was well received. But more important, it taught me about being creative enough to let go of things and look for something different if the need arises.

"I was fully prepared to let it go," Jim reflects. "I think that's part of what gives successful businesses their edge. I am constantly on the lookout for something new and better that will increase the effectiveness of our company. There's not a lot of room for nostalgia in business, unless it reflects solid business principles. So I guess it's a tightrope. I want the heritage of proven methods with the freedom to explore the new, all undergirded by letting things go when their creative effectiveness has worn thin."

Great teams constantly assess what is working and what isn't in order to maintain their cutting edge and maximize effectiveness. "If it ain't broke, don't fix it" is just as important as "If it ain't working, toss it."

Be More Creative Than Predictable

Why would a team work at being more creative than predictable? The obvious reason is that it keeps you from growing complacent. "We've always done it this way" has its place, but if it becomes a smoke screen that keeps people from moving into new areas, it should be addressed quickly.

In education there is a concept known as *creative dissonance.* It is built on the premise that some of the best learning takes place after the student has entered an uncomfortable situation. Consider your high-school English teacher's pronouncement: "George Orwell's *Animal Farm* is not just a story about pigs and ducks hanging around the barnyard. There is a deeper level to the book that gives it even greater meaning. See if you can find it." Knowing there is a meaning between the lines but not yet knowing what it is creates an attitude in some students that could be expressed as, "I must know what the hidden meaning is!" That dissonance, that unresolved tension, sets them up for more intense learning. The learning might not have occurred if the question had not been raised.

The same principle can be applied to business. Raising questions about the way we do things in order to move us from a place of complacency to a more creative place should be seen as a welcome addition to our day-to-day operations. Creativity, though immediately uncomfortable to some, can yield high results for a hardworking team.

Don't be afraid to ask the hard questions. Sometimes it's the only way to push your team out of being predictable and take advantage of the opportunities new ideas can provide.

- Would you describe your team as creative or predictable?
- What are some of the advantages of being a more creative team?
- Do you see the contributions made by all the members of your team, including those who are offstage and behind the scenes?

- How comfortable are you with tossing out an idea or practice that no longer works? Do you tend to hold on to things too long, saying, "We've always done it this way"?

Nine

Unity: We Are One in Our Performance

You may not know it, but you are walking around every day with one of the richest illustrations of effective teamwork. Take a moment to stand in front of a mirror to see what I am talking about.

It's your body!

Think about it. The body is a beautiful metaphor for an effective team, all parts working together toward a common goal: life.

The body is one unit that is made up of many parts, just like an athletic team or a symphony orchestra or a family. Most of us tend to think of our body as one big thing until something comes along that draws attention to a particular part. Admit it now; you don't think about your teeth all that much until you are sitting in the dentist's chair. Or you really didn't pay that much attention to your fibula until you broke it skiing. You'd probably never think about your elbow were it not for the crazy bone!

The point is, all these body parts join together to work as one. Several of them are at work right now to facilitate the reading of these words.

So what gives the human body unified effectiveness? I can break it down into four points:

WE ARE DIVERSE

All of our body parts belong to the same body, yet each of them is very different from the others. You wouldn't want your hands attached to your ankles in order to walk. You wouldn't want your ears responsible for your ability to see.

We are all very different, yet that diversity is what makes us work. Think about the level of effectiveness on your team. Your team wouldn't be as good as it is without the diversity of its members.

- Do I really believe what I read in the chapter about respect? Am I committed to it?
- What are some concrete ways I can express appreciation to my team for their diversity?
- What can I do to encourage even greater diversity of ideas and attitudes in my team?

WE ALL HAVE A SPECIALTY

Imagine your body has called a team meeting in the conference room. That's right—all the different body parts have the ability, in this imaginary scenario, to express thoughts and feelings. The body parts leader calls the meeting to order. (By the way, who is running your meeting—your brain? your heart? your stomach?)

The first speaker on the agenda is one of your feet. "I hate being the foot!" it gripes. "I have to live down here in this stinkin' sock and shoe all day. Everyone looks at the hands and oohs and aahs about how nice they are and how beautiful and grand they are when they gesture to underscore what is said. Hey, don't forget, if it wasn't for me, you wouldn't be standing there having that conversation!"

All attention is now given to the ear, and it proceeds to make the same case. "Why can't I be the eye? No one ever pays any attention to me. No one ever looks at me! When is the last time you were implored, 'Look me in the ear when I'm talking to you'? The eye gets all the glory! It's right smack in the center of the face, while I am hovering over on the side. It's just not fair!"

Silly as this story seems, there is a point. Every one of us is special because we all have a specialty. Have you ever tried getting by without your feet? It's pretty difficult. For some of us, just the thought of stubbing a toe is agony. Feet are on our body for a specific reason, to carry out a specialized task. It's the same with our ears. Have you ever noticed after a flight that your ears didn't pop during the descent? It's difficult to hear, and that changes everything! Our ears are on our body to accomplish something different from our eyes. It is a vital task, no less important and no more important than any other body part's function.

- First of all, am I convinced that I have a specialty? What is it?

- Next, how convinced am I of my team's individual specialties?
- How have I affirmed this principle on my team?
- Has any particular team member been overlooked in this process?

We Complement One Another

Third, *we complement one another.* That means we all fit together like pieces from the same puzzle. Effective teamwork occurs when we find our place in the puzzle and join the other pieces to create the total picture—the finished puzzle. My part in the puzzle is of equal value to your part. I am no better than you, nor are you better than I. We complement each other.

- Does my team look like a puzzle—in the good sense?
- What am I doing to encourage my team members to complement each other?
- Do we honestly believe that no one is better than another and that no one is worse? What needs to be done to reinforce this maxim in our team's makeup?

We Are One

You don't want your body parts acting independently of each other. You want your body parts all cooperating for the good of the team—your whole body. When you're driving your car, you want the eyes scanning the road ahead, the hands operating the steering wheel, and the right foot pressing the gas and brake pedals. This is no time for a wild streak of independence. We're all in this together.

If I don't build my team on the principle of respecting the team's diversity, specialties, and complementary nature, I am cooking with a recipe for disaster. It is only a matter of time before the team is fragmenting because the respect for each member, so vital for the team's health and survival, is missing.

- Is my team working together as one unit?
- How can I encourage individual team members to express their strengths while at the same time working together as a unit for the good of the team?
- What is a single goal that I can use to unify my team?

A UNIFIED TEAM

There's an additional aspect to the Carnegie Hall story I've waited until now to share. The concert was a wonderful, once-in-a-lifetime experience. I don't know what the kids in the choir thought about it, but I know every mom and dad in the hall will remember it.

The high-school choir was on a roll. As I already mentioned, the high schoolers performed classical pieces, contemporary pieces, songs in English, and songs in foreign languages. Each number seemed to outdo the previous one. The only downside was the constant attack of buttons as they popped off parents' puffed-up chests throughout the hall. We couldn't have been prouder.

As the concert moved to its conclusion, the choir began a song familiar to all of us in the audience. What happened next was so spontaneous, so natural, it was beyond scripting. Without any prompting by the conductor, the parents joined with the choir and began singing the song. It started rather softly, but before long we were singing at the top of our lungs. I recall the conductor glancing nervously over his shoulder as this noise from behind him began to swell. Our kids stared at us in disbelief.

Ultimately, the conductor gave in to our insistence. We were singing, and we weren't going to stop until the song was over. He continued to direct the choir but turned so we could see him as well. With a grand, bold movement of his long arms, he invited us to stand and officially join the choir. We were on our feet in an instant. It seemed unimportant at the time whether one knew how to sing or not. We knew the words of the song, and that was enough. I have few memories that equal the exhilaration generated in that concert hall at that moment.

When the song ended, being shy, retiring types, we remained on our feet and applauded wildly, essentially giving ourselves a standing ovation. It was one of those ovations that never seemed to end—at least I'm sure the conductor felt that way! We clapped and clapped with no intention of sitting down. We wanted the evening to last forever.

But eventually it had to come to a close. After a long and hearty standing ovation, we finally took our seats so the concert could move on to its scheduled conclusion.

"Well, that was really something!" the conductor announced.

Giddy as schoolchildren, we looked at one another and giggled excitedly. Yes, that was something; we had just turned a five-hundred-voice choir into a twenty-five-hundred-voice mass chorale. And we were proud of ourselves.

"Actually, I'll let you in on a little secret. I was preparing to invite you to stand and join us," the conductor confided, "but it is obvious you needed no coaxing from me."

We laughed and nodded, still thoroughly energized by the event.

"There is a reason I wanted you to join in," the conductor continued. "Now each and every one of you can say in complete honesty, 'I sang in Carnegie Hall.' "

It took only a second for that thought to sink in. Once again we exploded into deafening applause, filled with gratitude over what had just transpired. In a wonderfully creative gesture, the conductor included us on his team. And using the gifts, the energy, and the enthusiasm we possessed, we gave it all we had. We became one voice, working together for the climax of the concert. It was a magnificent moment built around the power of unity.

And we were better as a result. That's what teamwork can do in your life.

THE CARNEGIE HALL EFFECT

I need to belong. I need to feel worthy. I need to feel competent. All three of those needs can be met in conjunction with an effective team.

I can get beyond the barriers of personal insecurity, unhealthy competition, lack of communication, and an unwillingness to change. In hurdling those roadblocks, I can move toward the great traits of an effective team.

I run my teams with the same respect I have for all the parts of the human body. I can recognize and celebrate my team's diversity, just as I do the amazing diversity we have in our families. I know the value of sacrifice, just as athletic teams see its value. And the creativity of a great choir and orchestra inspires me toward my own creativity in the way I run my team.

Put it all together, and we are one. Above all else, the unity of a team is its greatest strength. I've started referring to it as the Carnegie Hall Effect. All of us connected together on a smooth-running team are like a choir and an orchestra playing the most famous musical venue in the world. Ask any of your musician friends—getting an invitation to play Carnegie Hall is still the most desired envelope in the mail. It means you've arrived. You are at the top of your game. You are the master of your craft. It's a musician's Super Bowl.

And that's what your team can look and feel like. Going to work every day can feel like playing Carnegie Hall. Why? Because you are doing what you are meant to be doing. There's not much in the world that is more fulfilling than that.

So let's put into practice what we have learned. Some of us might need the plane to land first, but once we get off this jet, let's get busy creating an effective team.

- What is the most important truth you learned through this book?
- What is the one thing you will begin acting on immediately as a result of reading this book?
- If you had to make one change in the way you run your team, what would that one change be?

Notes

1. Wilbur Schramm, "How Communication Works," in *The Process and Effects of Mass Communication,* ed. Wilbur Schramm (Urbana, IL: University of Illinois Press, 1955), 4–8, quoted in Raymond S. Ross, *Essentials of Speech Communication* (Englewood Cliffs, NJ: Prentice-Hall, 1979), 9.

2. The concepts in this section come from a great book on change: *Taking the Fear Out of Changing* by Dennis O'Grady (Holbrook, MA: Adams Media, 1993).

3. Robyn Norwood, "Eagles' Reid Feeds Off L.A. Roots," *Los Angeles Times,* December 2, 2000.

4. Mike Shanahan and Adam Schefter, *Think Like a Champion: Building Success One Victory at a Time* (New York: HarperBusiness, 1999), 138.

About the Author

Bill Butterworth's extraordinary ability to blend humor, storytelling, wisdom, and practicality has made him one of the most sought-after corporate speakers throughout North America. Through his wit, warmth, insight, and realism, he brings help and hope to audiences everywhere.

Bill taught at the college level for thirteen years and was a counselor for six years prior to his current passion for motivating men and women in the workplace. He was awarded the Hal Holbrook Award by the International Platform Association, whose past and present members include Mark Twain, Theodore Roosevelt, Bob Hope, and Elizabeth Dole. Bill is one of the select few members to be named a top-rated speaker by the association.

Since 1988, Bill has traveled full time, speaking to hundreds of audiences as small as eighteen and as large as eighteen thousand. His Fortune 500 clients include:

Allstate
American Express
Bank of America
BlueCross BlueShield
Boise Cascade
Century 21 Real Estate
Citibank
DaimlerChrysler
First Data Corporation
Ford Motor Company
Hilton Hotels
Johnson Controls

MassMutual
Parker Hannifin
PNC Bank
SBC
T. Rowe Price
Verizon
Wachovia Bank
Walt Disney Company

Bill has also addressed twenty-six of the teams in the National Football League as well as more than a dozen teams in Major League Baseball. Bill's complete client list reads like a who's who of corporations, associations, educational agencies, and professional sports teams.

In 2004 Bill established the Butterworth Communicators Institute (BCI) to help train men and women to find their speaking voice and raise their speaking ability to the next level. The overwhelmingly positive response to BCI has been gratifying as students maximize their skills through this intensive yet intimate three-day workshop.

In addition to the On-the-Fly series, Bill has written more than a dozen books, including *The Promise of the Second Wind* and *When Life Doesn't Turn Out Like You Planned.*

For more information about Bill Butterworth, please visit his Web site at www.BillButterworth.com.